Samurai COLORING BOOK

One of the most popular writers in nineteenth-century Japan was Bakin, who lived from 1767 to 1848. His most famous book, *The Tale of the Eight Dog Heroes of Satomi*, or *Satomi Hakkenden* in Japanese, was published in 106 installments from 1814 to 1842. Fans waited eagerly for the publication of each new chapter of the exciting story, which tells of eight heroes, each with the word for "dog" (in Japanese, *inu*) in his family name. (In Japanese, the family name comes first, with the personal names after it.) The eight heroes are as brave and loyal as faithful dogs. They use a combination of sword fighting, magic, and strategy to defeat the enemies of the Satomi clan, and after many adventures, they are finally successful.

Just as best-selling books today are made into movies, *The Eight Dog Heroes* became a Kabuki play that was produced many times with different actors. Many artists drew designs for woodblock prints showing the poses and expressions of the actors and the colorful costumes and stage sets. When you color the pictures, you can follow the colors they used or try new combinations. The last page is blank so that you can draw your own picture of a thrilling scene that you would enjoy seeing on stage or in a movie. What costumes would you design for the heroes of your favorite adventure story?

Pronunciation:

Bakin = Bah-KEEN   Satomi = Sah-TOE-mee   Hakkenden = HOCK-ken-den

inu = EE-noo   Kabuki = kah-BOO-kee

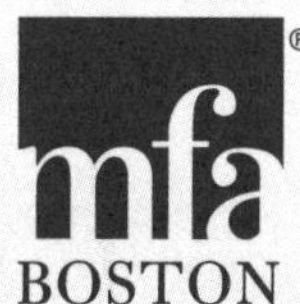

Pomegranate Kids™

All works of art are from the collection of the Museum of Fine Arts, Boston, William Sturgis Bigelow Collection. Unless otherwise specified, each image is a detail from a woodblock print *(nishiki-e)*; ink and color on paper; vertical ōban. All artists are Japanese.

1. Utagawa Kunisada I (Toyokuni III; 1786–1864). Publisher: Jōshūya Kinzō. *Actors as Inuzaka Asa Keno (R) and Inuta Kobungo (L).* Edo period, 1847–52. Vertical ōban diptych. 11.43766a-b.
2. Utagawa Kunisada II (Toyokuni IV; 1823–1880). Publisher: Tsutaya Kichizō (Kōeidō). *Actor Asao Okuyama III as Neruda Gobaiji,* from the series *The Book of the Eight Dog Heroes (Hakkenden inu no sōshi no uchi).* Edo period, 1852 (Kaei 5), 12th month. 11.39145.
3. Utagawa Kuniyoshi (1797–1861). Publisher: Shimizuya. *Actor Bandō Shūka I as Inuzaka Keno,* from the series *The Lives of Eight Brave and Loyal Dog Heroes (Giyū hakken den).* Edo period, about 1848–49 (Kaei 1–2). 11.38029.
4. Utagawa Kunisada II. Publisher: Tsutaya Kichizō. *Actor Nakamura Tamasuke I (Nakamura Utaemon III) as Moriguchi Kurō, a valiant retainer of Satomi (Satomi yūshin),* from the series *The Book of the Eight Dog Heroes (Hakkenden inu no sōshi no uchi).* Edo period, 1852 (Kaei 5), 10th month. 11.39114.
5. Utagawa Kunisada II. Publisher: Tsutaya Kichizō. *Actor Ōtani Tomoemon IV as Yayayama Hikiroku,* from the series *The Book of the Eight Dog Heroes (Hakkenden inu no sōshi no uchi).* Edo period, 1852 (Kaei 5), 12th month. 11.39120.
6. Isshūsai Kunikazu (active about 1848–1868). Publisher: Ishikawaya Wasuke (Ishiwa). *Awa Province: (Arashi Kichisaburō III as) Inuyama Dōsetsu,* from the series *The Sixty-odd Provinces of Great Japan (Dai Nippon rokujū yo shū).* Edo period, about 1857–61 (Ansei 4–Bunkyū 1). Woodblock print *(nishiki-e)*; ink, color, and metallic pigment on paper. Horizontal chūban. 11.37828.
7. Isshūsai Kunikazu. Publisher: Ishikawaya Wasuke. *Mino Province: (Mimasu Daigorō IV as) Takenaka Shigeharu and (Ōtani Tomomatsu I as) Maeda Inukiyo,* from the series *The Sixty-odd Provinces of Great Japan (Dai Nippon rokujū yo shū).* Edo period, about 1857–61 (Ansei 4–Bunkyū 1). Woodblock print *(nishiki-e)*; ink, color, and metallic pigment on paper. Horizontal chūban. 11.37833.
8. Utagawa Kunisada II. Publisher: Tsutaya Kichizō. *Actor Iwai Tojaku I (Iwai Hanshirō V) as Inue Shinbei Masashi,* from the series *The Book of the Eight Dog Heroes (Hakkenden inu no sōshi no uchi).* Edo period, 1852 (Kaei 5), 9th month. 11.39137.
9. Utagawa Kunisada II. Publisher: Tsutaya Kichizō. *Actor Sawamura Sōjūrō V as Inumura Daikaku Masanori,* from the series *The Book of the Eight Dog Heroes (Hakkenden inu no sōshi no uchi).* Edo period, 1852 (Kaei 5), 9th month. 11.39133.
10. Utagawa Kunisada II. Publisher: Tsutaya Kichizō. *Actor Ichikawa Danjūrō VIII as Satomi Yoshinari,* from the series *The Book of the Eight Dog Heroes (Hakkenden inu no sōshi no uchi).* Edo period, 1852 (Kaei 5), 12th month. 11.39162.
11. Isshūsai Kunikazu. *Actors Arashi Kichisaburō III as Inuta Kobungo and Nakamura Daikichi III as the courtesan Kakitsu (R), and Arashi Rikan III as Inuzuka Keno (L),* in Act 7 of the play *Yatsu no Hanafusa.* Edo period, 1857 (Ansei 4), 1st month. Vertical chūban diptych. 11.20662a-b.
12. Toyohara Kunichika (1835–1900). Publisher: Sanoya Tomigorō (Kinseidō). *Actor Kawarazaki Gonjūrō I as Inukai Genpachi,* from the series *The Eight Dog Heroes of Satomi (Satomi hakkenshi no uchi).* Edo period, 1866 (Keiō 2), 8th month. 11.40591.
13. Kinoshita Hironobu I (active about 1851–1870). Publisher: Kinokuniya Yasubei. *Actors Jitsukawa Enjaku I as Inuzuka Shino (R) and Ichikawa Ichijūrō II as Inukai Genpachi (L)* in the Hōryūkaku scene of the play *Satomi Hakkenden.* Edo period, 1863 (Bunkyū 3), 9th month. Vertical chūban diptych. 11.35055-6.
14. Utagawa Kunisada I. Publisher: Ebisuya Shōshichi. *Actors Ichikawa Danjūrō VIII as Inuzuka Shino Moritaka (R) and Bandō Hikosaburō IV as Inukai Genpachi Nobumichi (L),* from the series *Eight Dog Heroes of Satomi (Satomi Hakkenshi no hitori).* Edo period, about 1847–50 (Kōka 4–Kaei 3). Vertical ōban diptych. 11.43770a-b.
15. Isshūsai Kunikazu. *Actors Arashi Rikaku II as Inuzuka Shino (R) and Arashi Kichisaburō III as Inuzuka Bansaku (L)* in the play *Hakkenden.* Japanese, Edo period, 1857 (Ansei 4), 9th month. Vertical chūban diptych. 11.35803a-b.
16. Utagawa Kuniyoshi. Publisher: Kagaya Kichiemon (Kichibei). *Actor Sawamura Tosshō as Inumura Kakutarō,* from the series *Actors as the Eight Dog Heroes ([Mitate] haiyū hakkenshi).* Edo period, 1831–42 (Tenpō 2–13). 11.38086.
17. Toyohara Kunichika. Publisher: Sanoya Tomigorō. *Actor Ichimura Kakitsu IV as Inuzuka Shino,* from the series *The Eight Dog Heroes of Satomi (Satomi hakkenshi no uchi).* Edo period, 1865 (Keiō 1), 12th month. 11.40595.
18. Ichiyōsai Yoshitaki (1841–1899). *Brothers (Kyōdai): Actors Onoe Tamizō II as Inuyama Dōsetsu (R) and Ichikawa Udanji I as Inukawa Sōsuke (L),* from the series *Matches for the Five Relationships (Mitate godō no uchi).* Meiji era, 1868 (Keiō 4/Meiji 1), 10th month. Vertical chūban diptych. 11.36067a-b.
19. Isshūsai Kunikazu. *Actors Arashi Rikan III as Inuzaka Keno (R) and Arashi Kichisaburō III as Inuta Kobungo (L)* in Act 6 of the play *Yatsu no Hanafusa.* Edo period, 1857 (Ansei 4), 1st month. Vertical chūban diptych. 11.35786a-b.
20. Isshūsai Kunikazu. *Actor Arashi Rikaku II as Inukai Genpachi* in Act 4 of the play *Yatsu no Hanafusa.* Edo period, 1857 (Ansei 4), 1st month. Vertical chūban. 11.37052.
21. Utagawa Kunisada II. Publisher: Tsutaya Kichizō. *Actor Iwai Kumesaburō III as the Shirabyōshi dancer Asakeno, actually Inusaka Keno Tanutoshi,* from the series *The Book of the Eight Dog Heroes (Hakkenden inu no sōshi no uchi).* Edo period, 1852 (Kaei 5), 10th month. 11.39155.
22. Ichiyōsai Yoshitaki. *Actor Arashi Rikan III as Inuzaka Keno* in the play *Yatsu no Hanafusa.* Edo period, 1857 (Ansei 4), 4th month. Vertical chūban. 11.35533.

Pomegranate Communications, Inc.
Box 808022, Petaluma CA 94975
800 227 1428
www.pomegranate.com

Pomegranate Europe Ltd.
Unit 1, Heathcote Business Centre, Hurlbutt Road
Warwick, Warwickshire CV34 6TD, UK
[+44] 0 1926 430111
sales@pomeurope.co.uk

Catalog No. CB107
Designed by Susan Koop
Printed in Korea

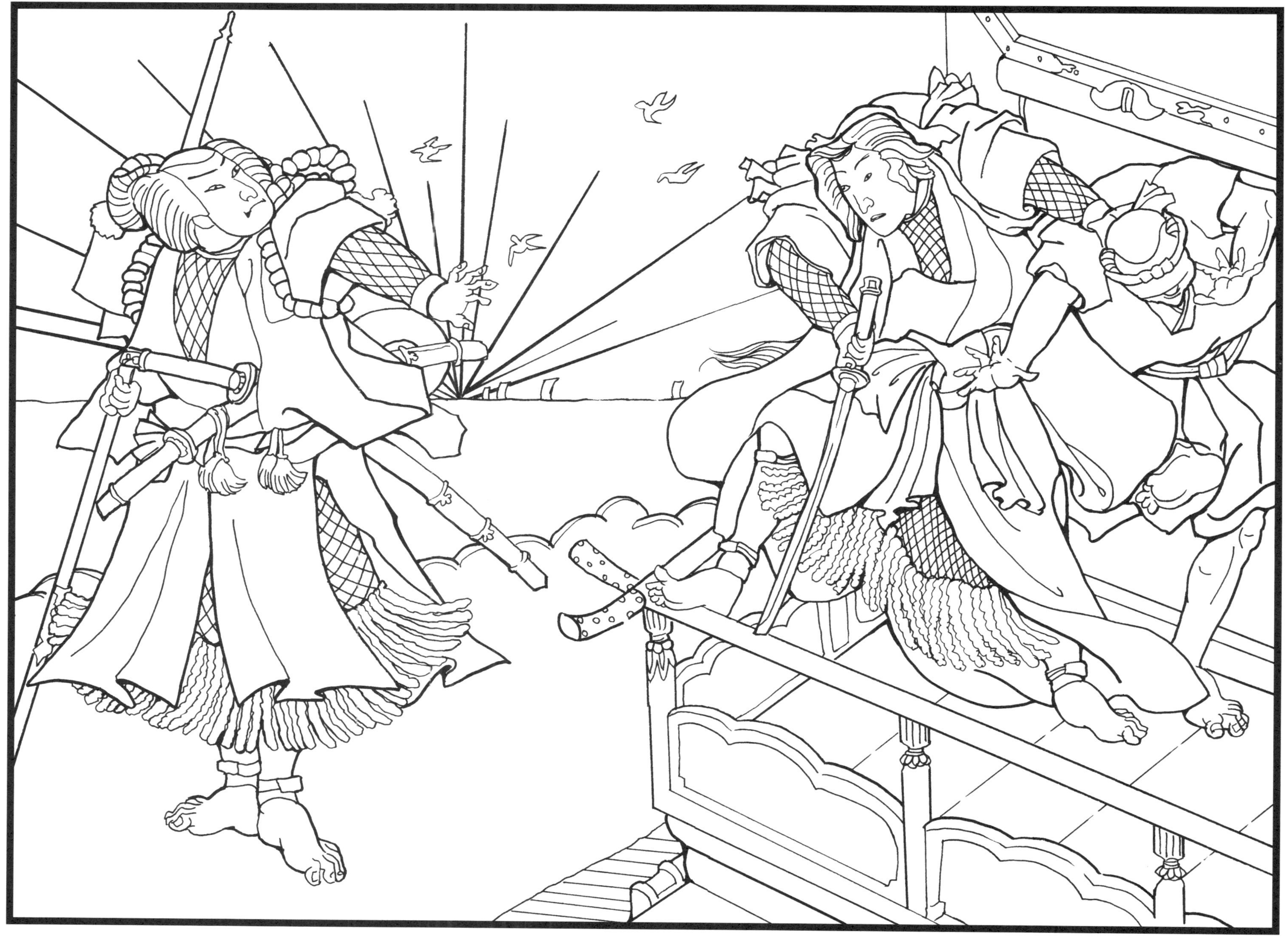

1.

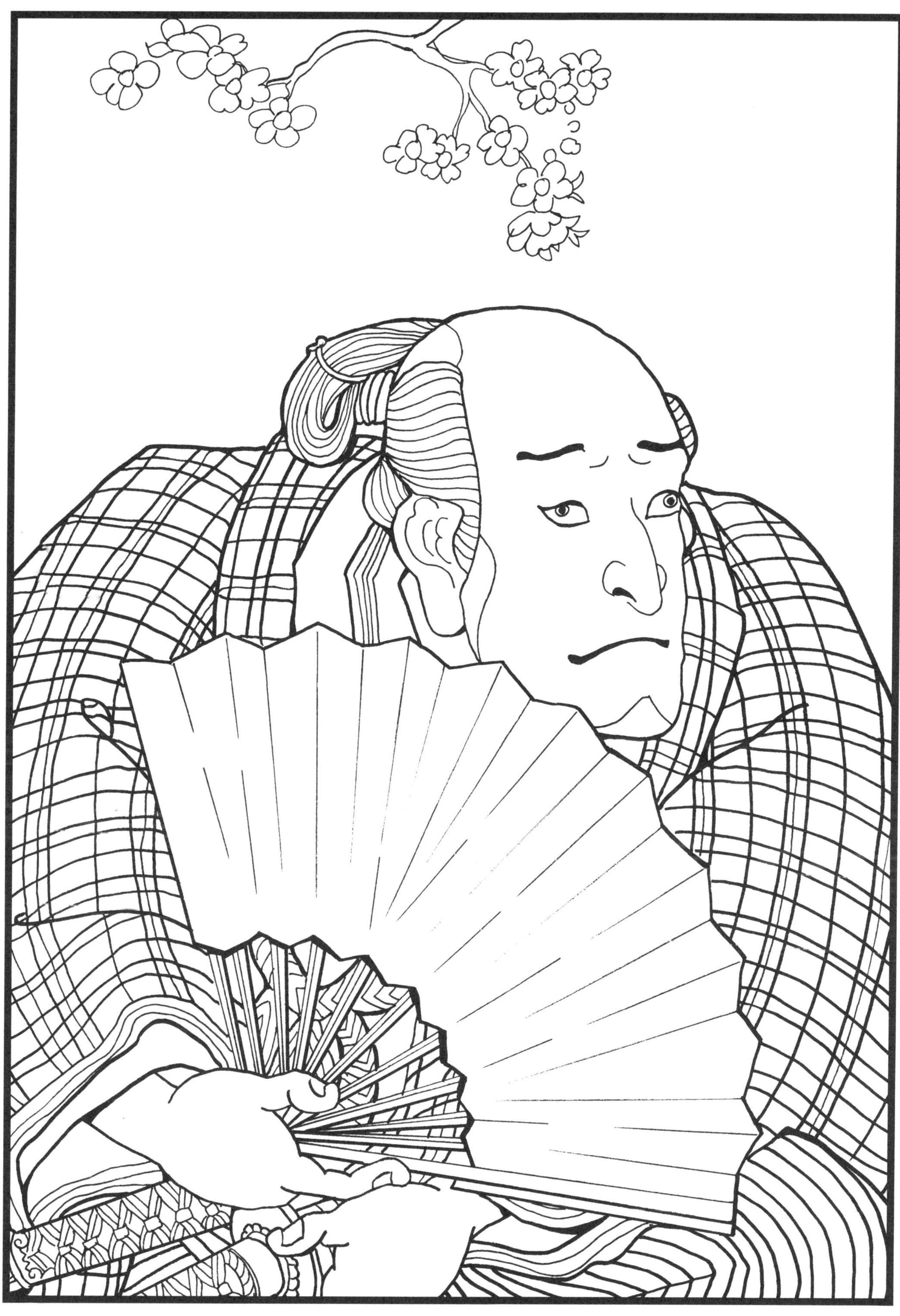

2.

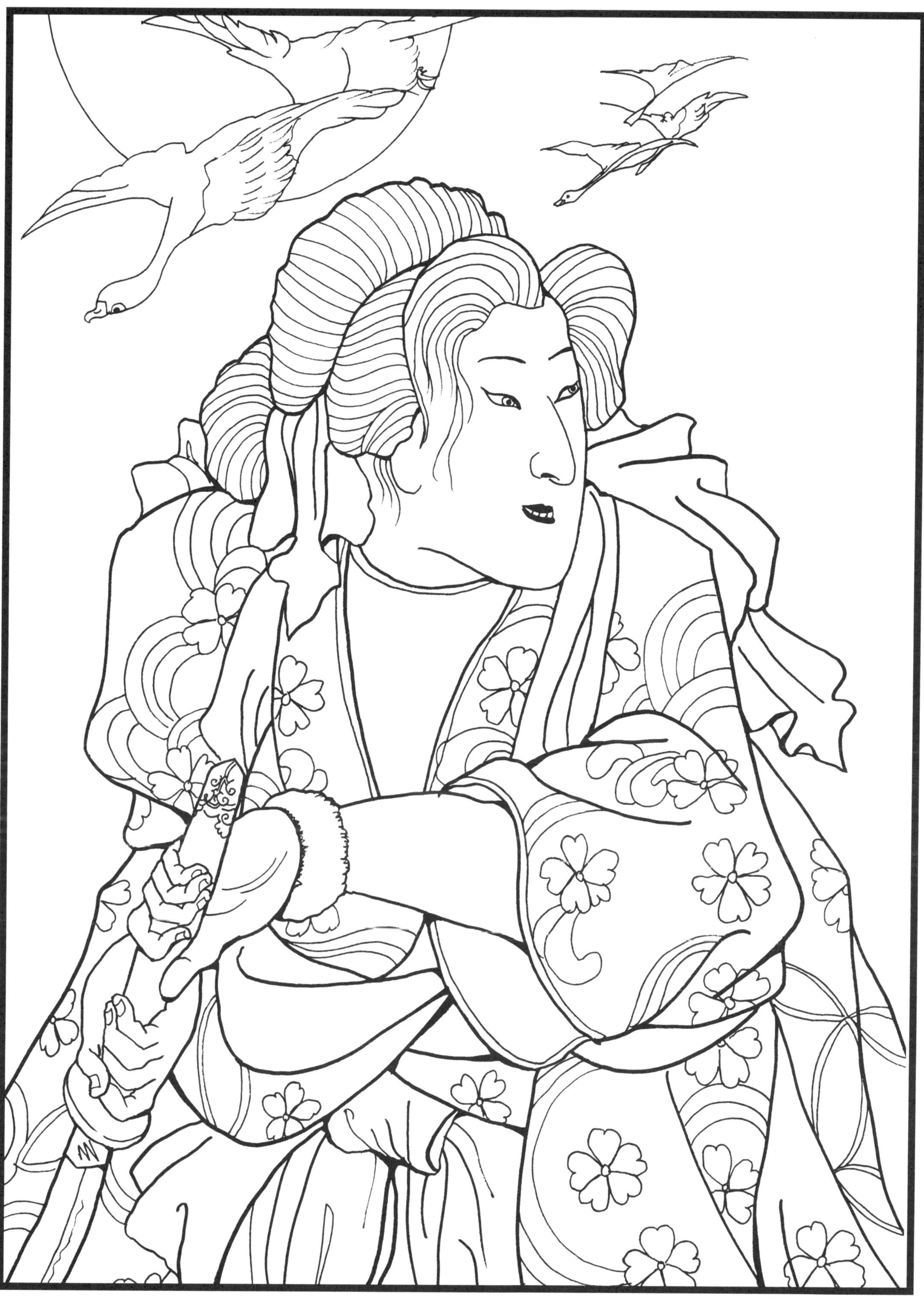

3.

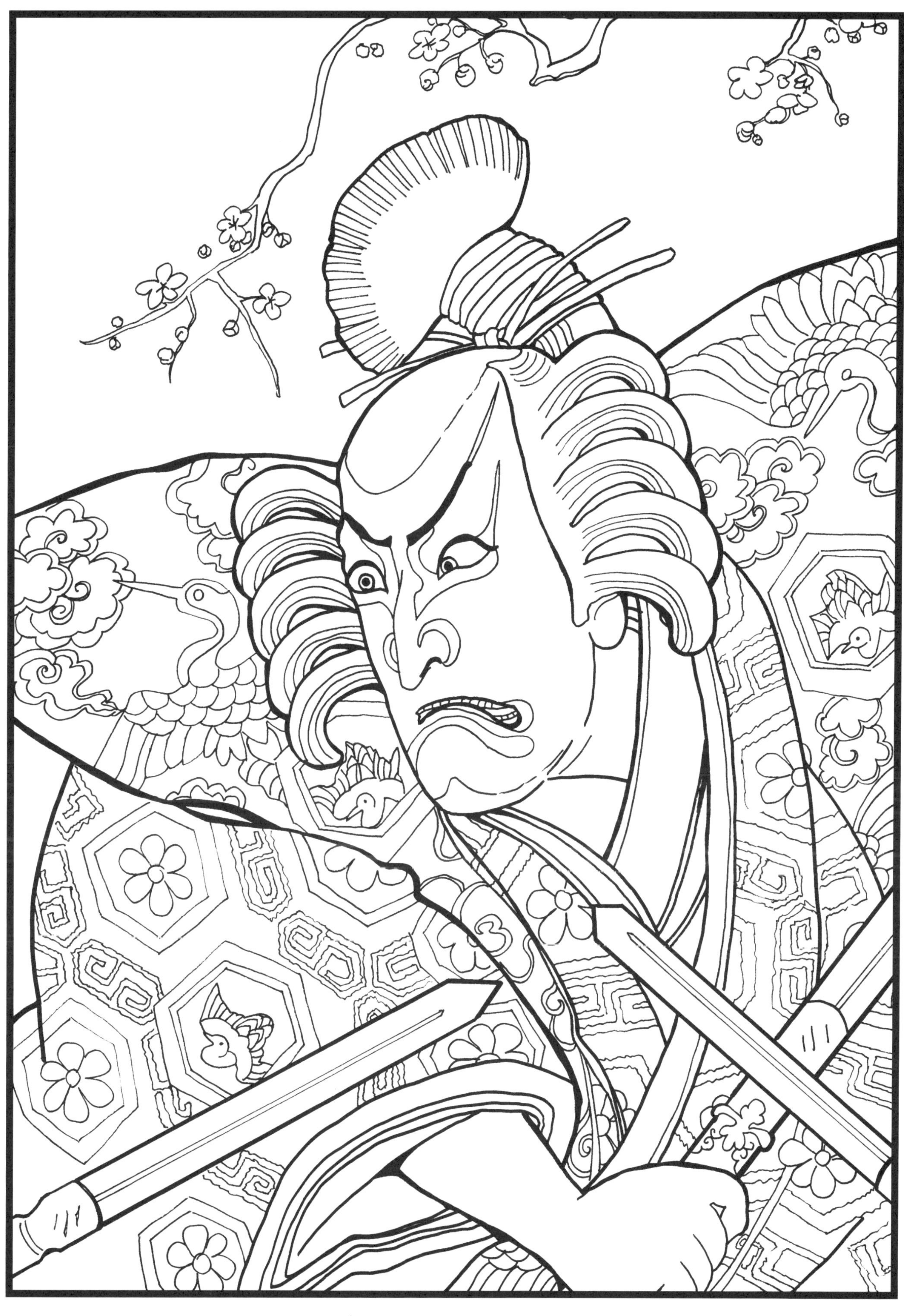

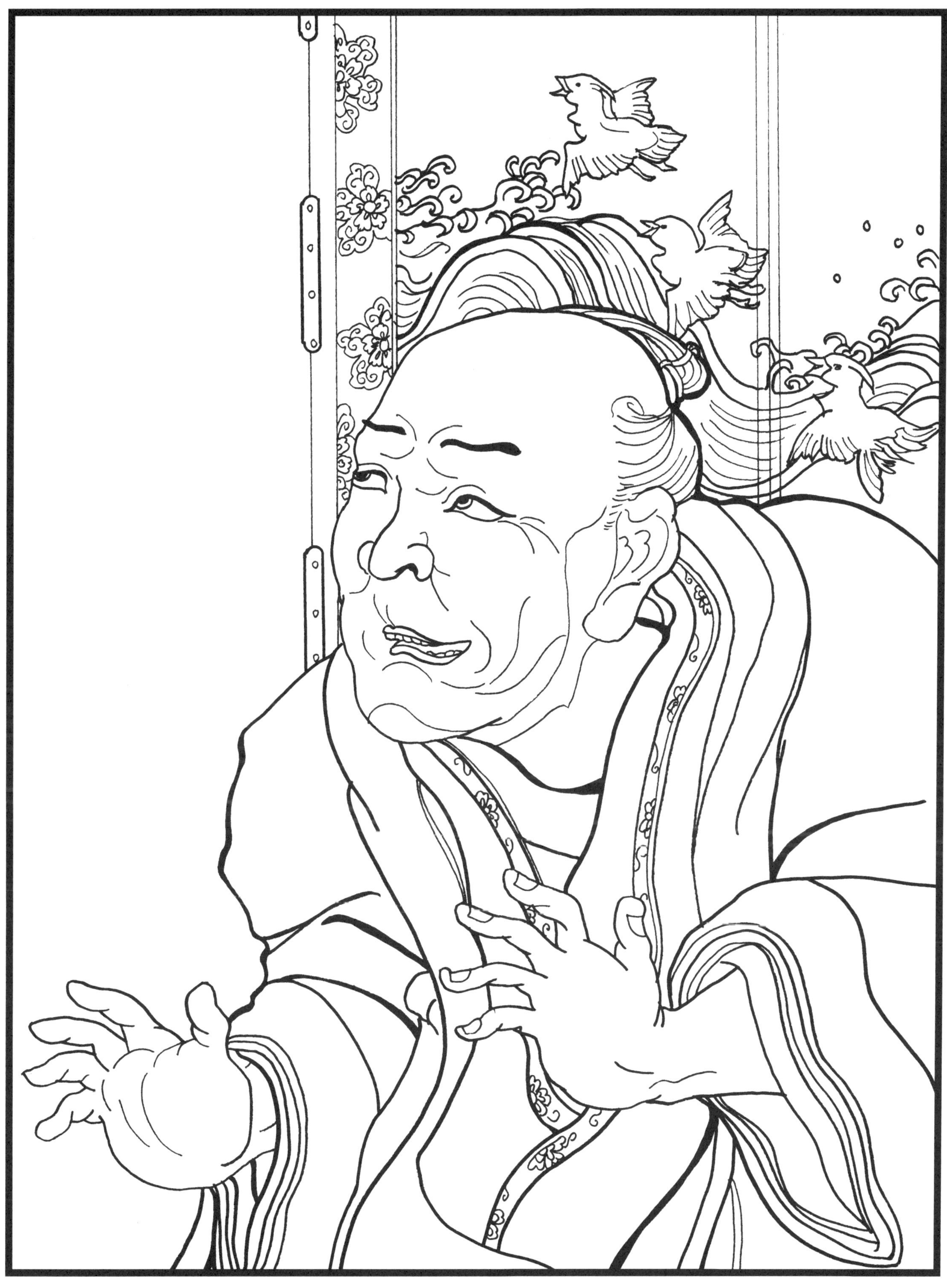

5.

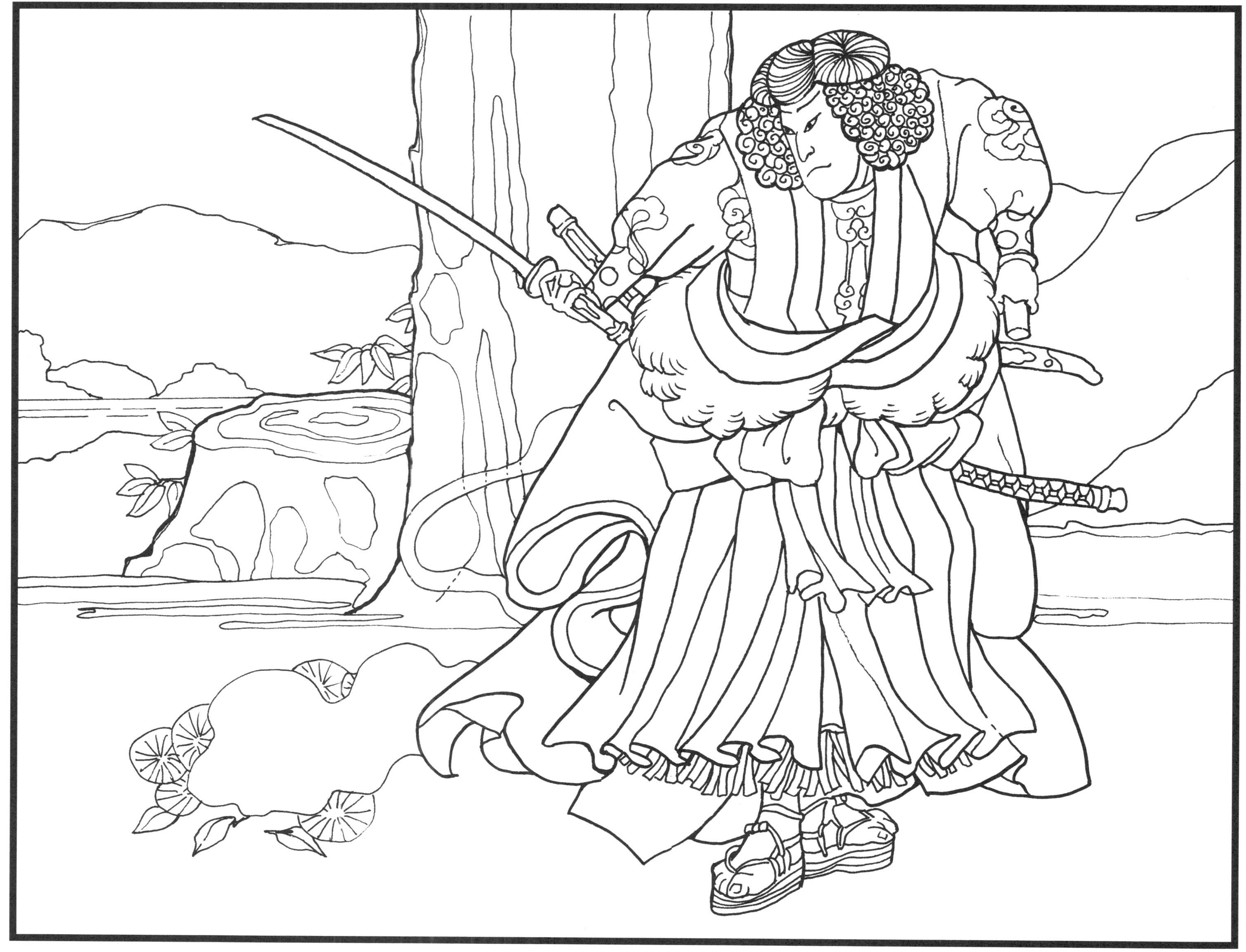

6.

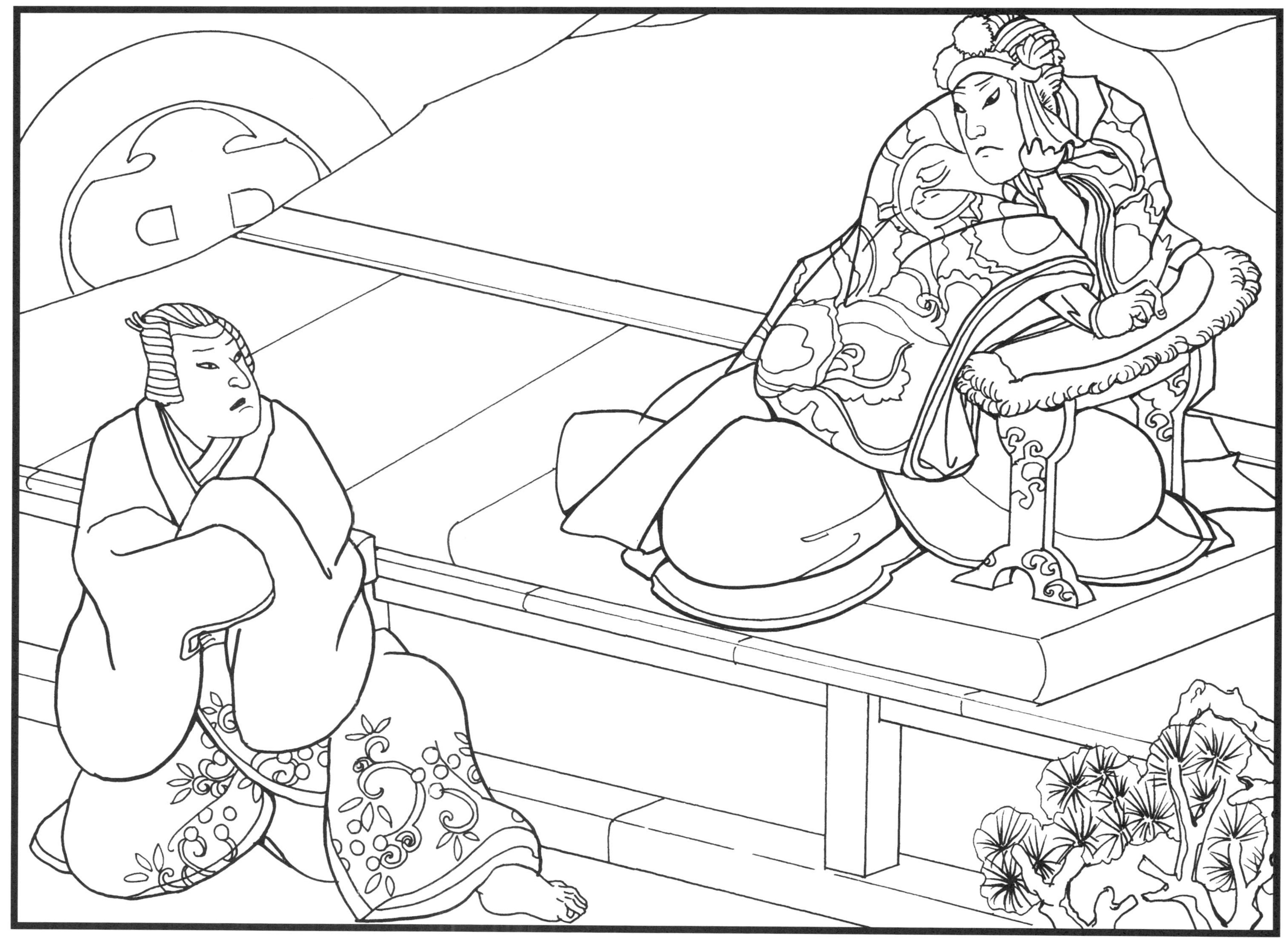

7.

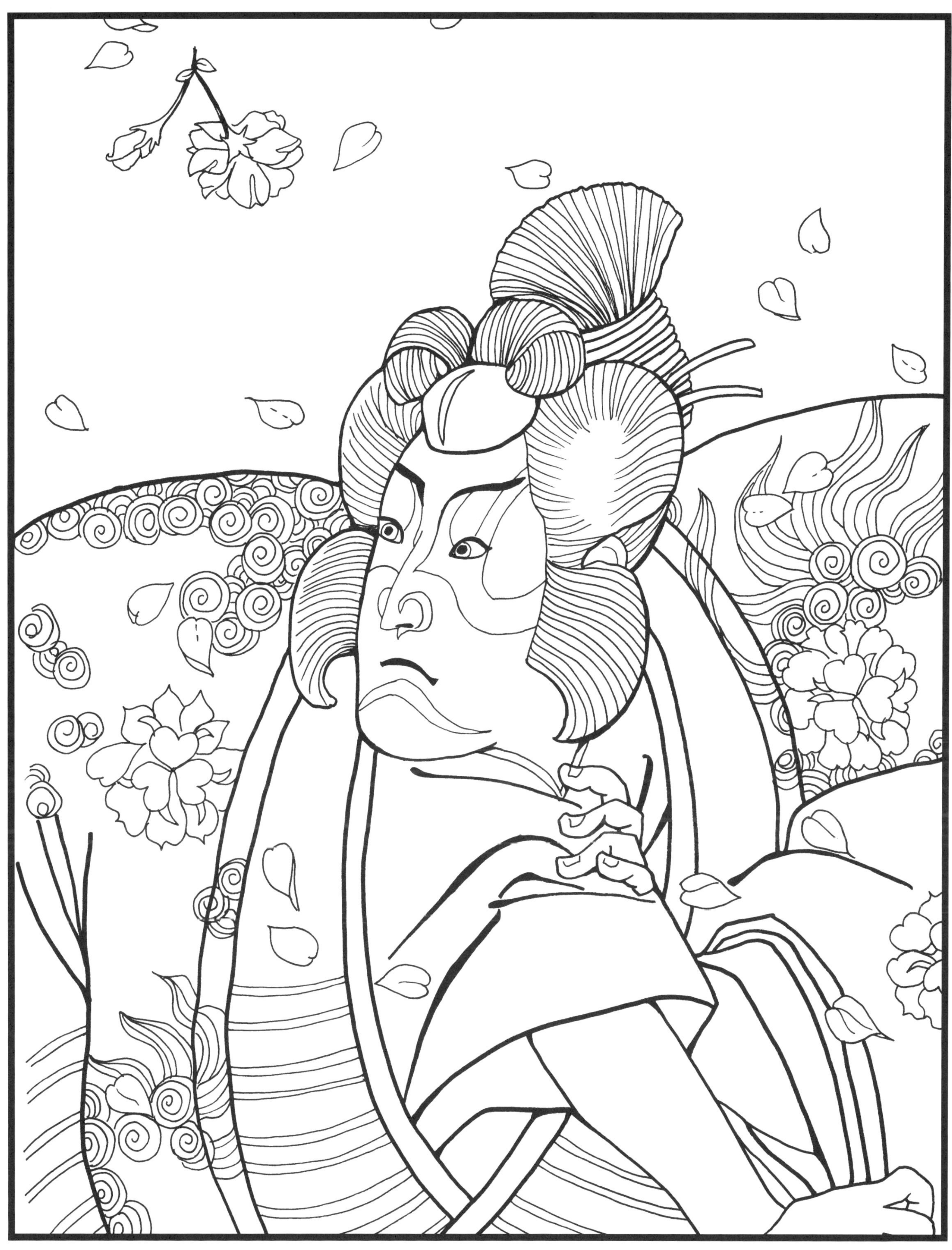

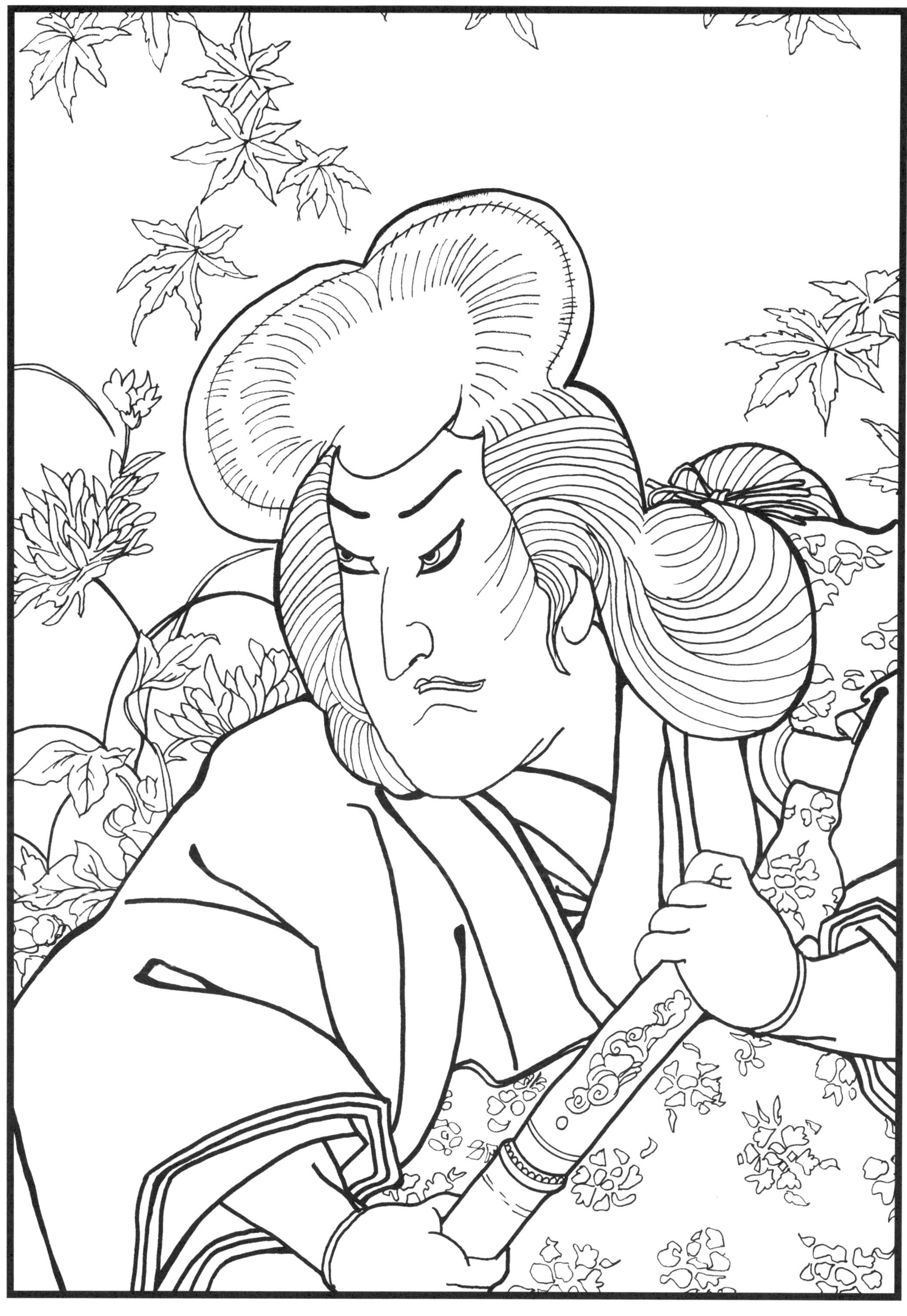

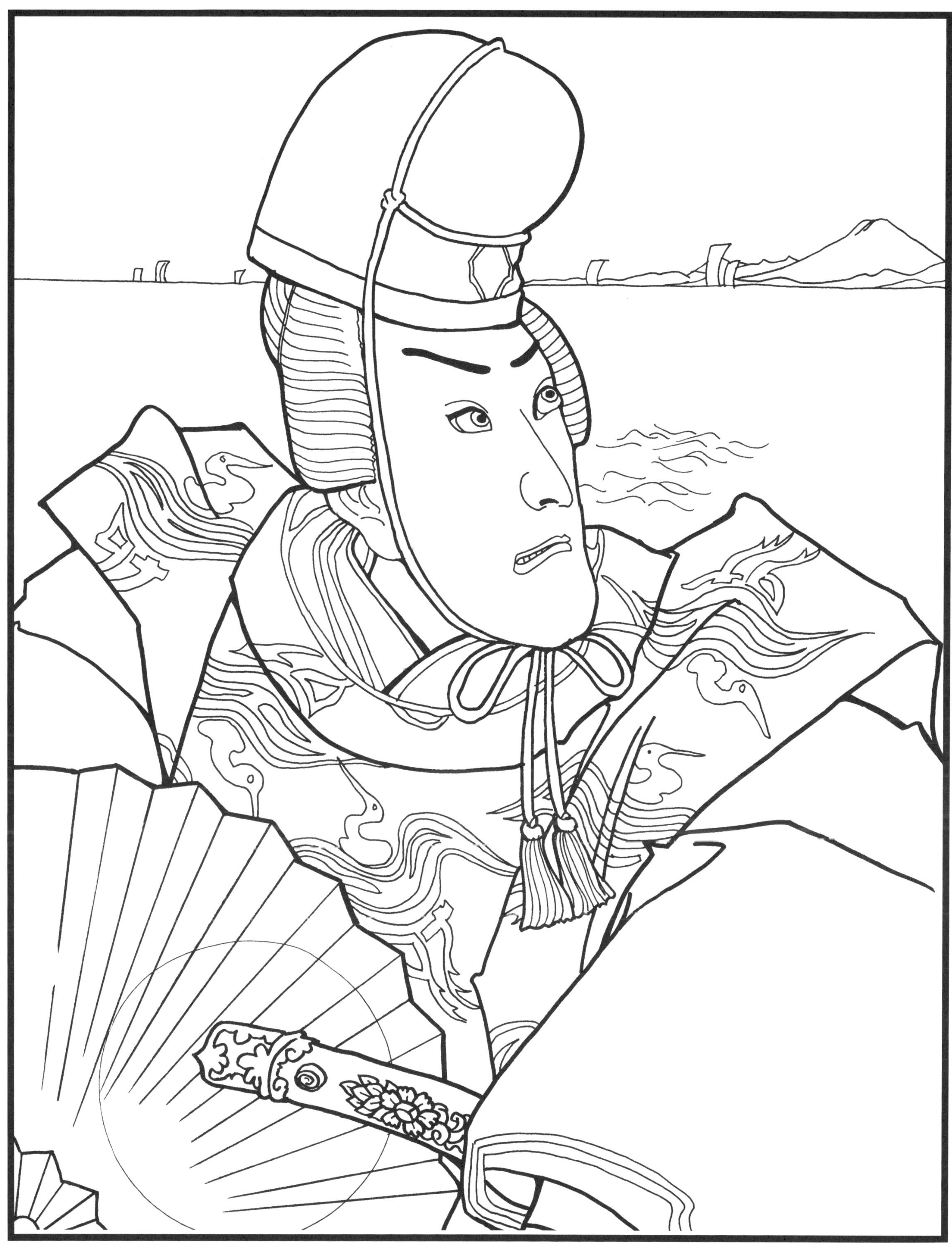

10.

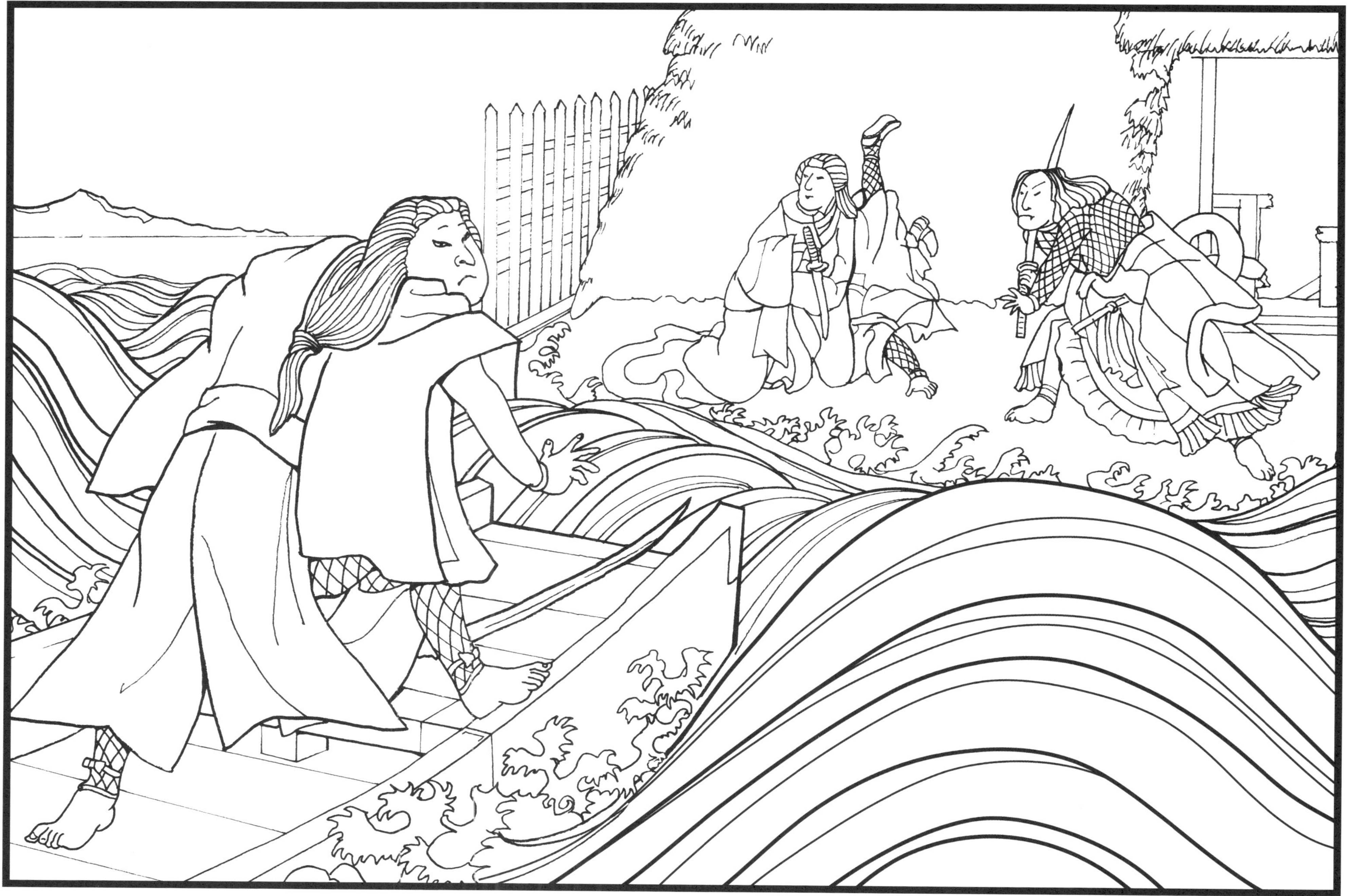

11.

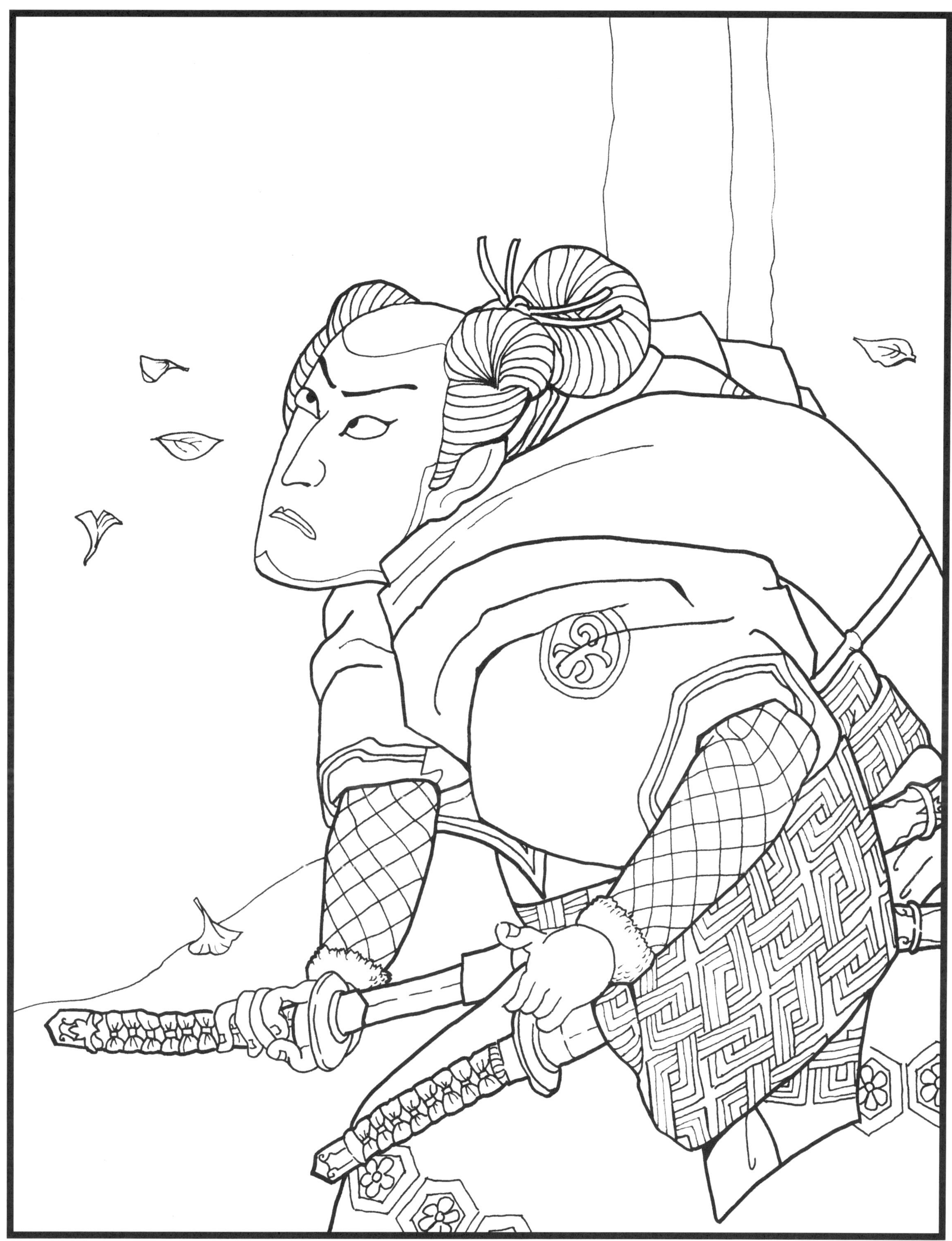

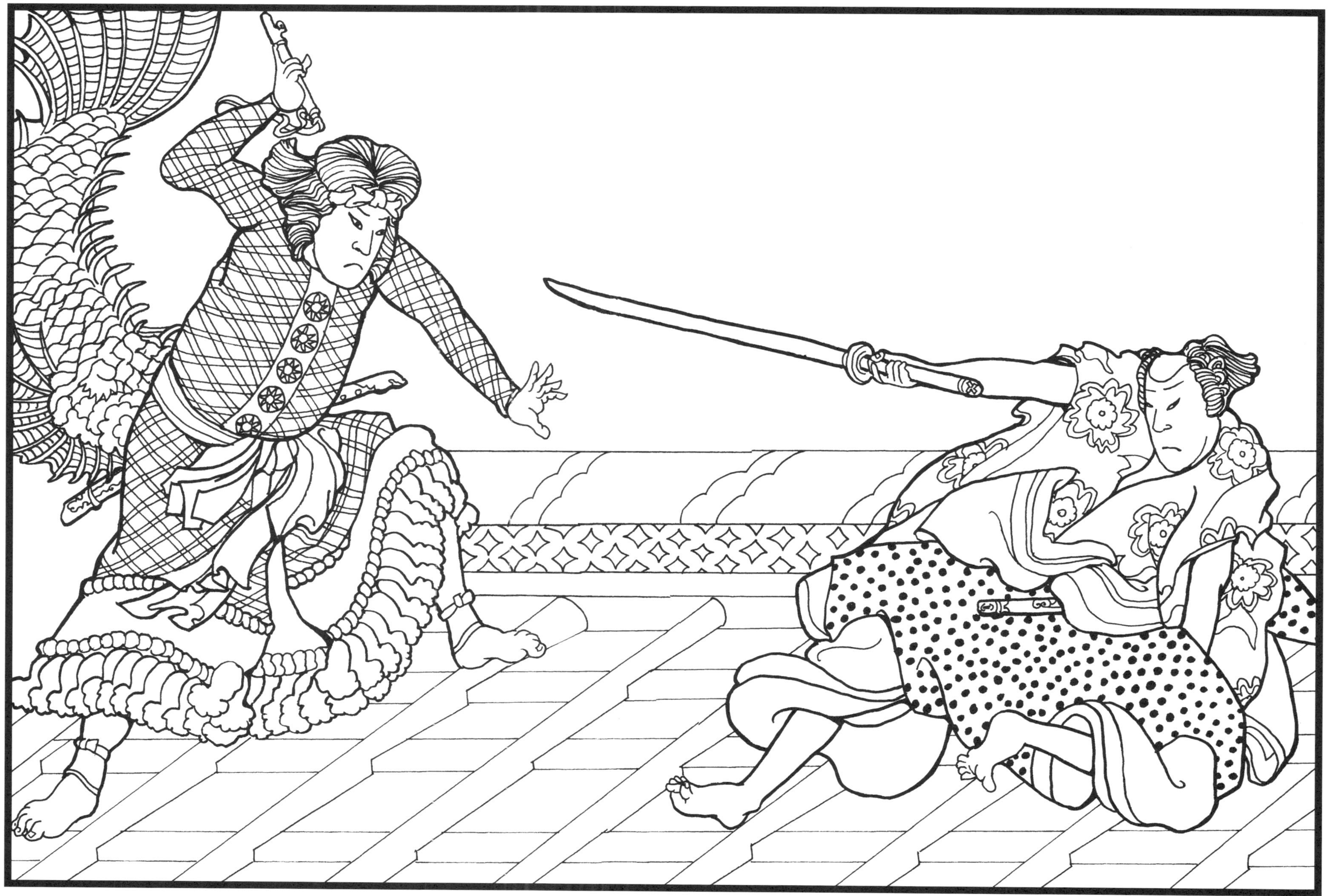

13.

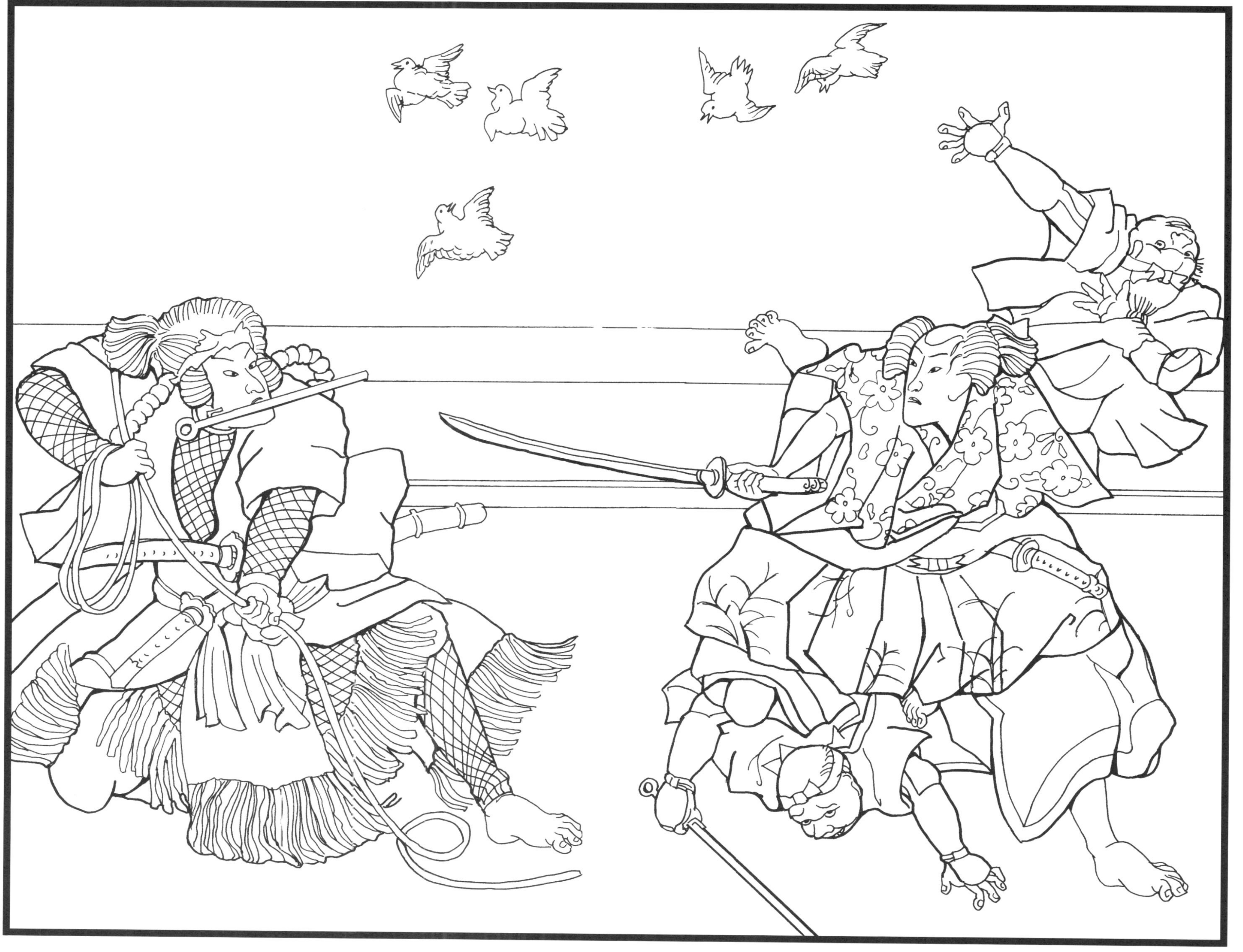

14.

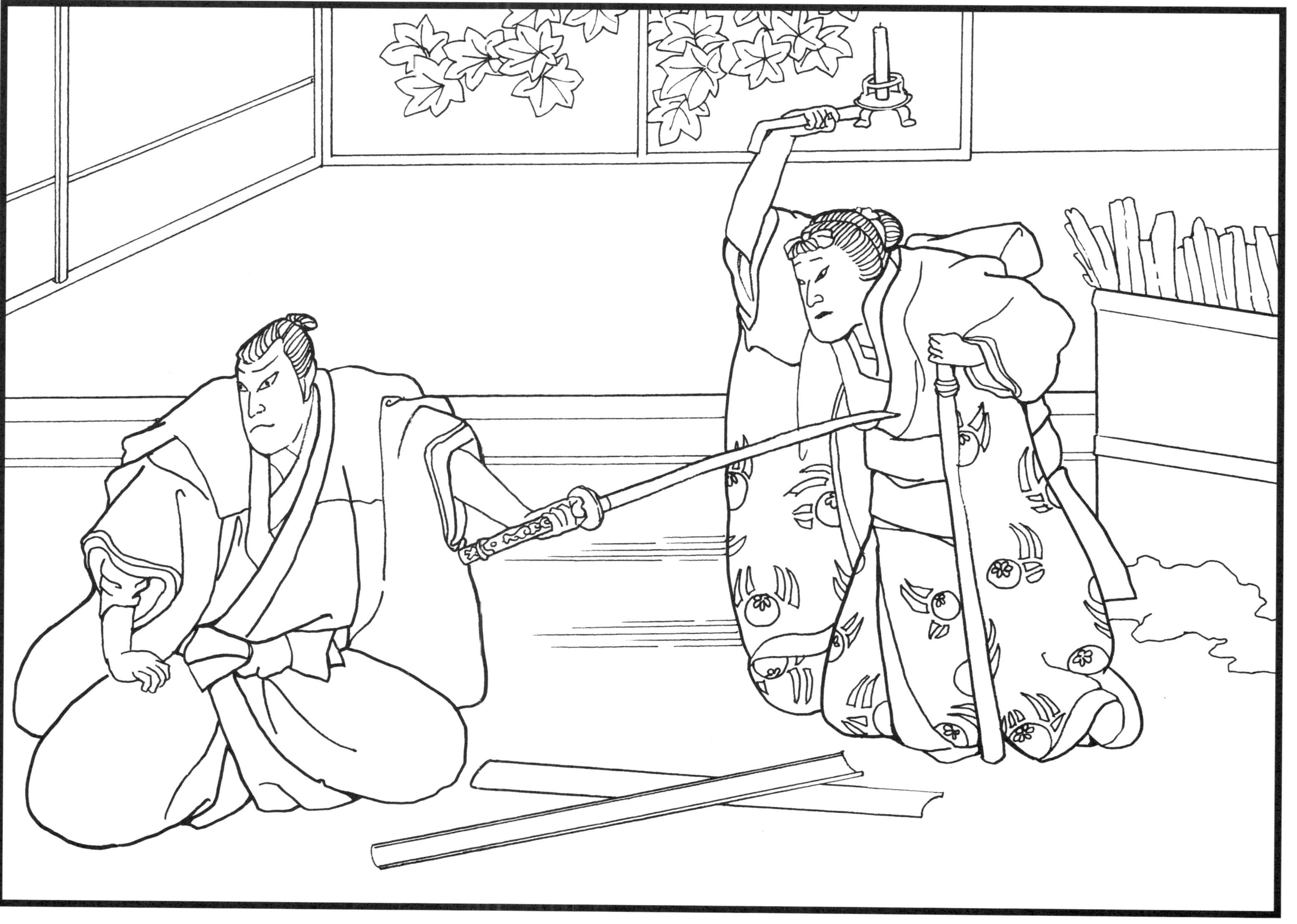

15.

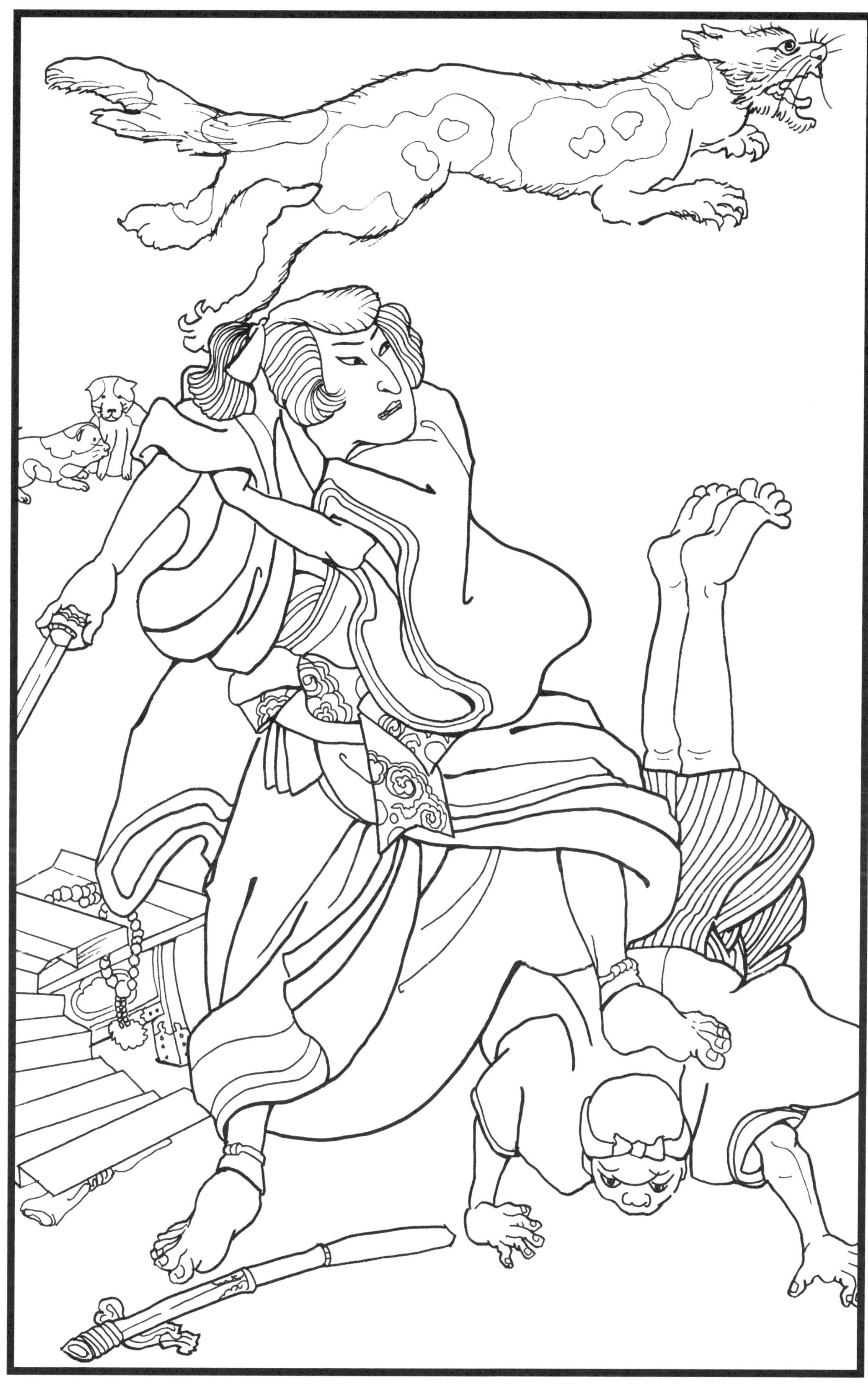

16.

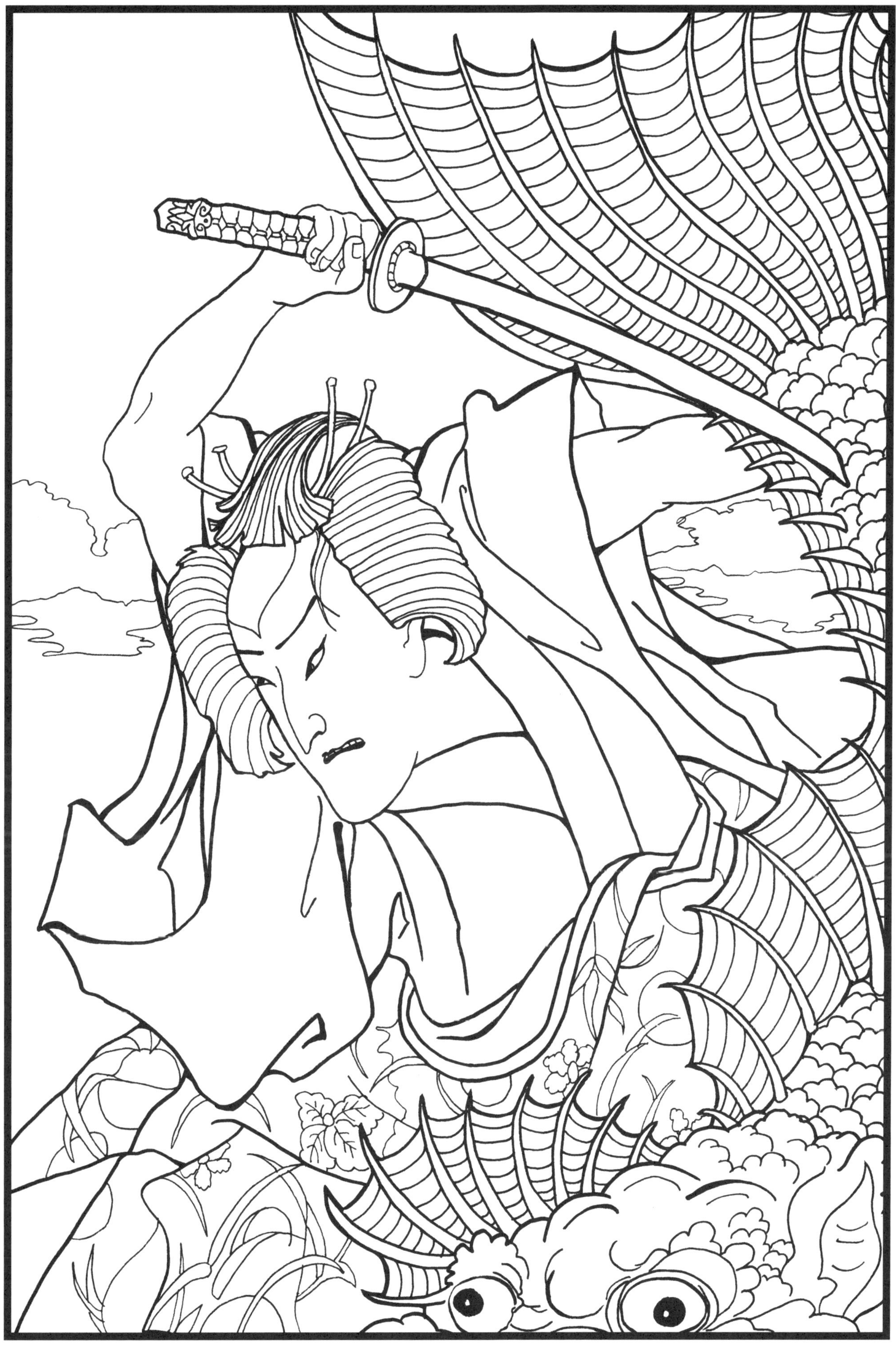

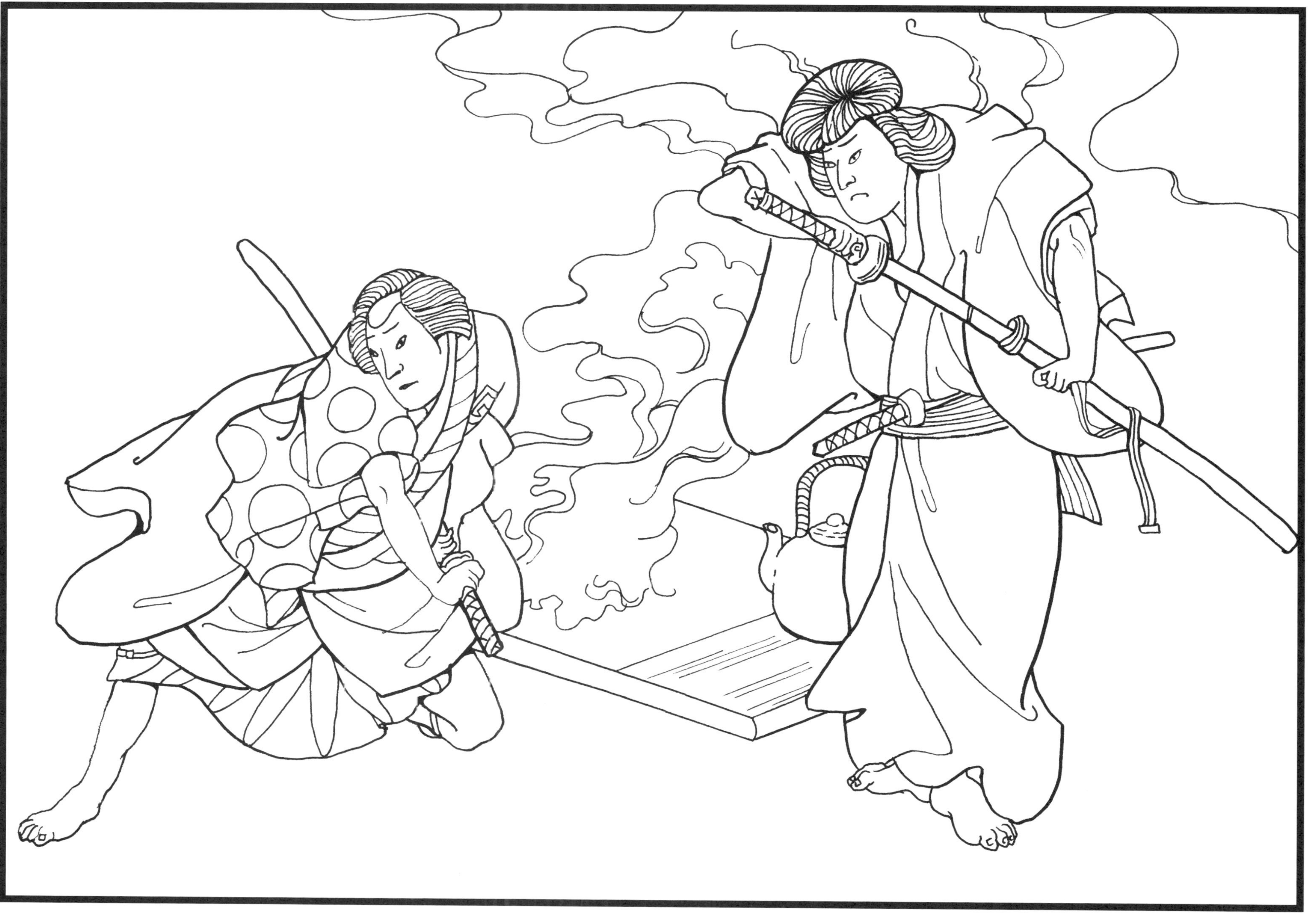

18.

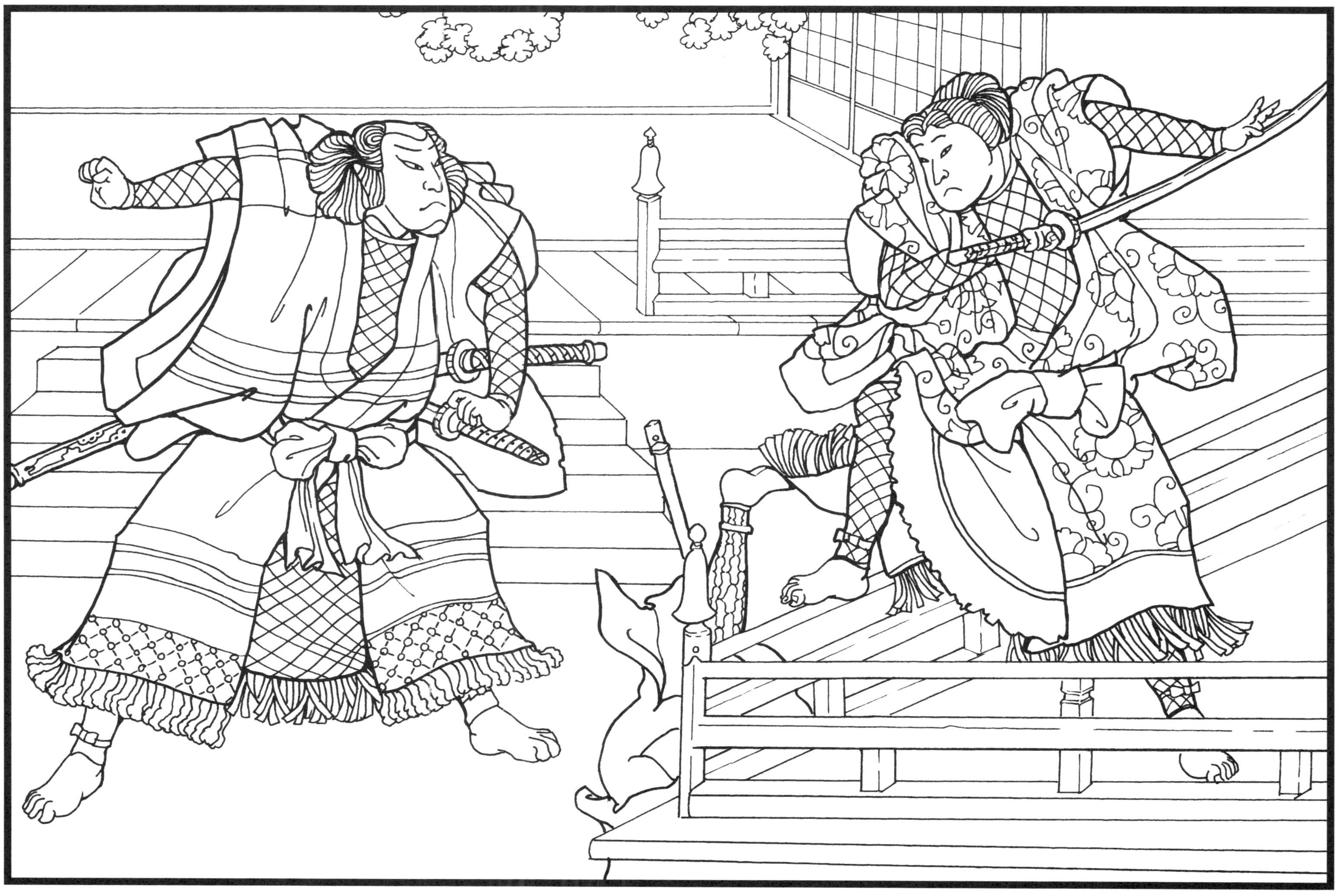

19.

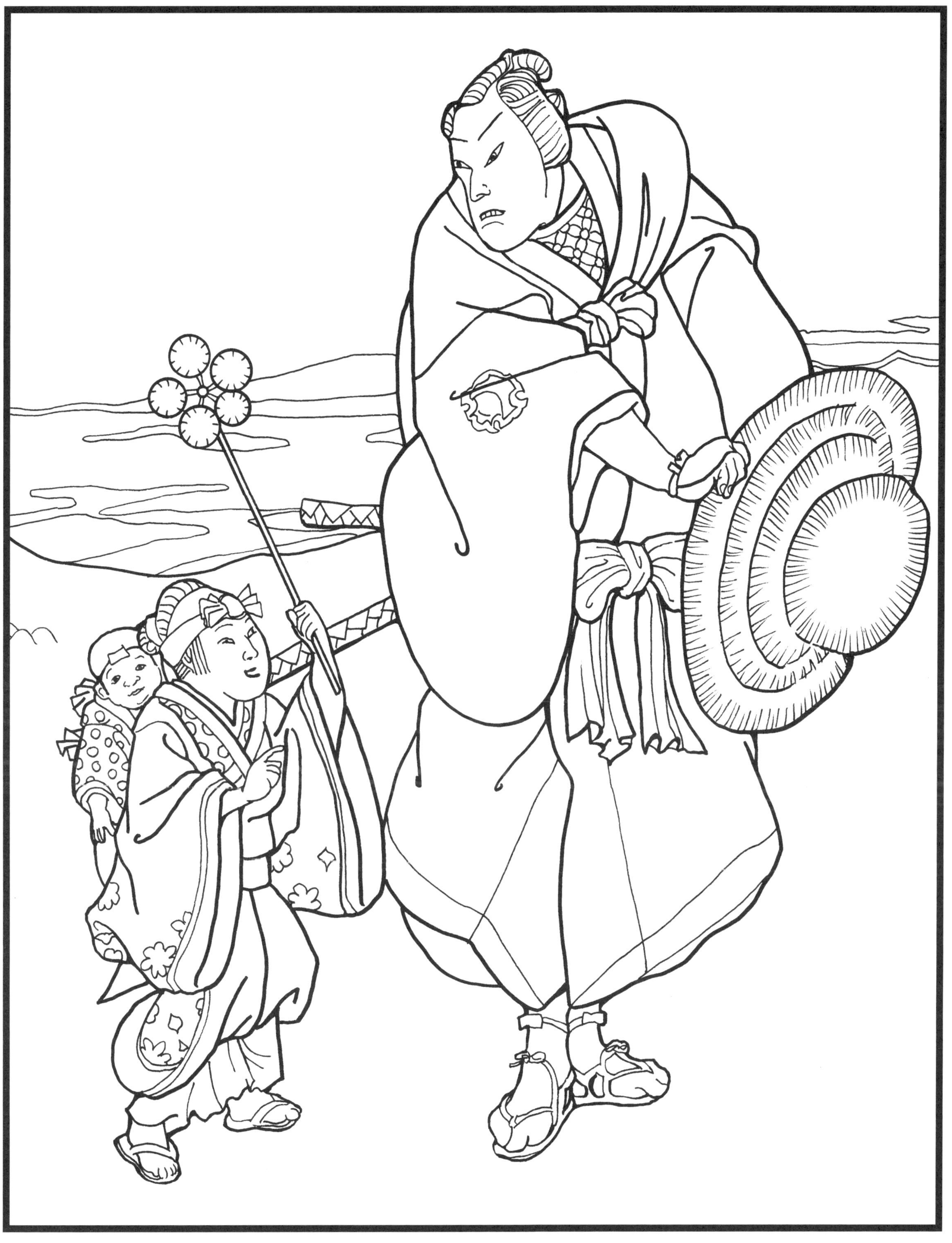

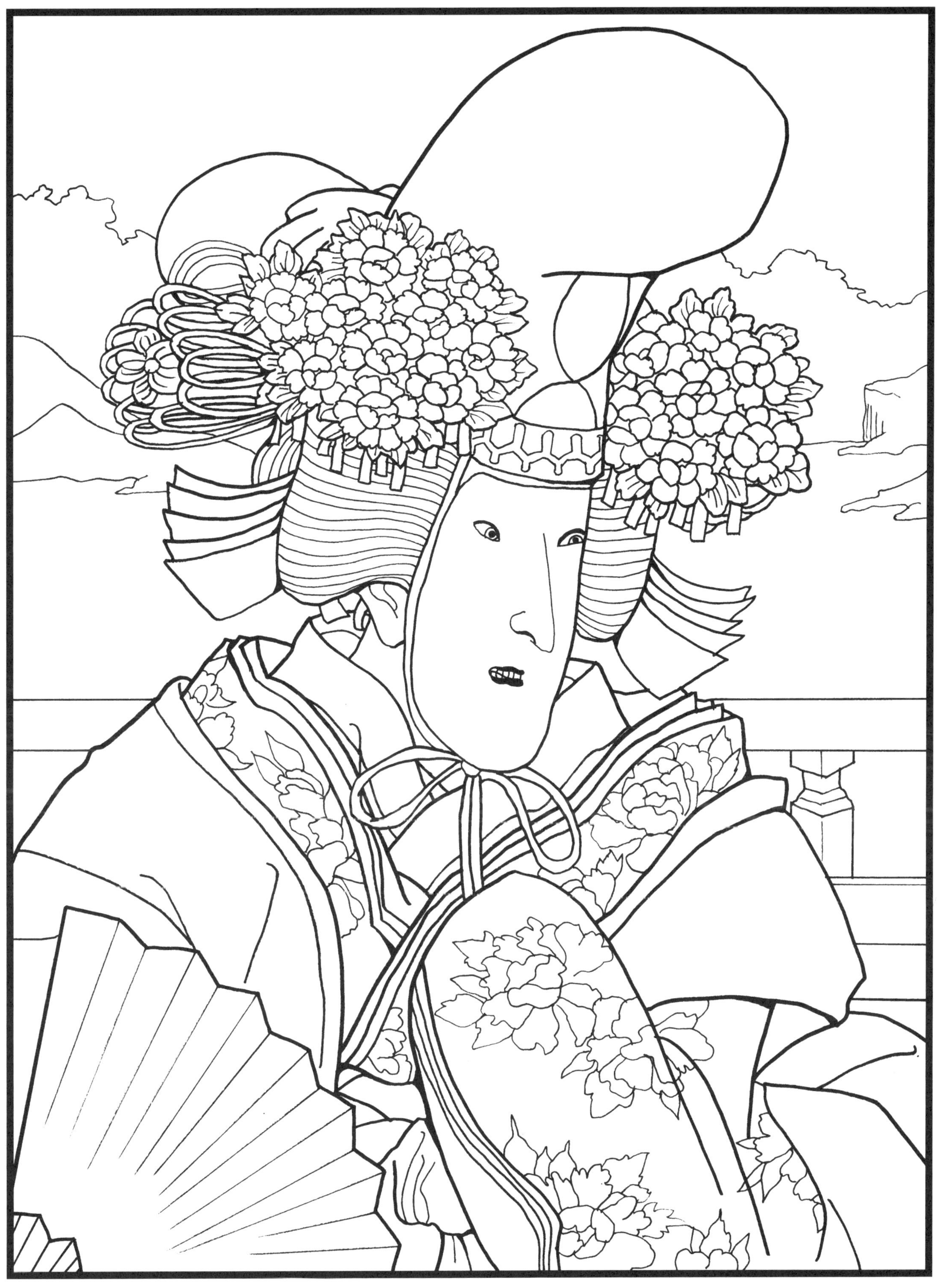

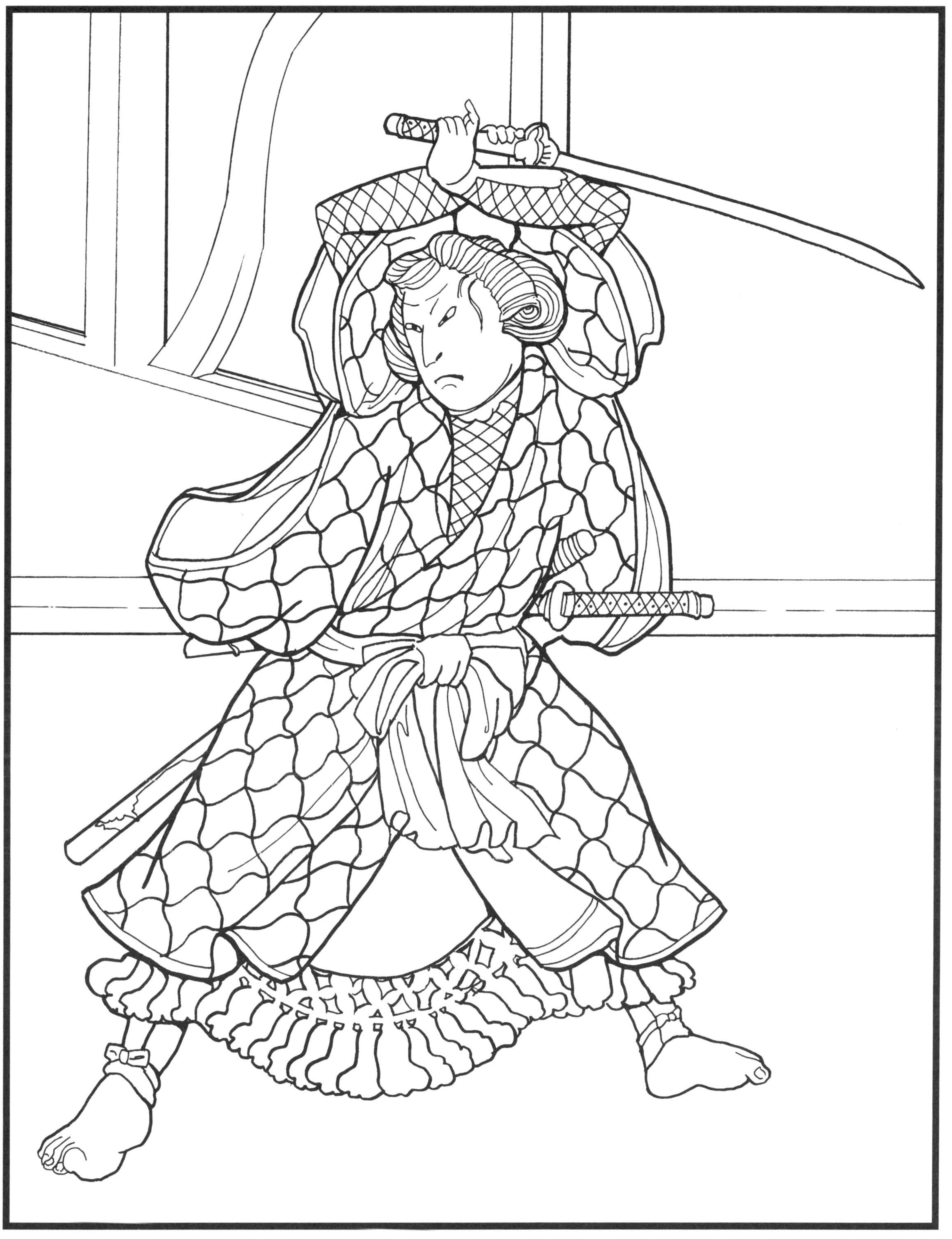

Draw and color your own picture here!